Thirty-One Prayers for my Husband

SEEING GOD MOVE IN HIS HEART

JENNIFER SMITH

AN *Unveiled Wife* RESOURCE

W9-BFJ-097

Thirty-One Prayers for my Husband

SEEING GOD MOVE IN HIS HEART

JENNIFER SMITH

AN Unveiled Wife RESOURCE

Thirty-One Prayers For My Husband
Seeing God Move In His Heart

Written By Jennifer Smith

Copyright © 2014
Smith Family Resources, Inc.

ISBN-13: 978-1490907550
ISBN-10: 1490907556

Book Website
unveiledwife.com/31prayersbook

Printed in U.S.A

CONTENTS

Seeing God Move

Philippians 4:6-7

"Do not be anxious about anything, but in everything by prayer and supplication with thanksgiving let your requests be made known to God. And the peace of God, which surpasses all understanding, will guard your hearts and your minds in Christ Jesus."

Introduction

Marriage is a beautiful reflection of God's incredible love story. A husband and wife reflect the covenant relationship of Jesus Christ and His bride, the Church. We are the Church! Jesus compassionately pursues each one of us. He has an intense desire to have an intimate relationship with us, regardless of our sin, faults, and failures. His love truly is unconditional and perfect.

As a wife there have been many moments where my love for my husband proved to be conditional. I wanted him to change for the better, I wanted him to be the man I knew he could be. However, my approach was wrong. I tried to get through to him and change his heart by pointing out his error and being overly critical, nagging, and manipulative. I have learned that this type of behavior, regardless of my intention, pushed my husband away from me. Realizing that my heart still desired the best for my husband, I went to God! I began to pray for my husband and the desires that filled my heart. I encountered something quite phenomenal...

I saw God move in my husband's heart!

This was far more powerful than trying to get my husband to change to do things my way. Instead I saw the Lord working in and through my husband, a beautiful occurrence that actually began changing me! As my husband drew closer to God, I began desiring what he had. I inevitably drew closer to God. My prayers also changed as my heart aligned with God's desires for our marriage. When I stopped nagging or complaining to God about my husband, and began praying for him in specific ways, God revealed a few things to me:

- I had issues that needed to be addressed in my heart.
- My focus switched from wanting my husband to change for me to wanting my husband to be transformed by God for His purpose.
- I discovered a need to pray over my marriage daily.
- I found power in prayer! God hears me and moves in both my husband and me.
- Thankfulness began to flow from my heart more than ever before, which changed my perspective about my marriage.

These were amazing findings that radically altered my perspective of marriage. Prayer has revolutionized my relationship with God and with my husband.

I have experienced so much growth in these important relationships that I wanted to share the value of prayer with you!

Prayer is a way to communicate with God. I wrote these thirty-one prayers to encourage you to pray for specific areas of your husband's life. I urge you to use these prayers as a guide, but also to include your own desires and hopes for your husband and marriage! Each day's topic may not apply perfectly to your husband's circumstances, but you can still use it to guide you as you add to each one your husband's needs. I believe these prayers will spark a passion in your heart to trust God, to lean on Him, and to experience more in your relationship with Him and with your husband.

As you submit your heart to God in prayer, you will see Him move in your husband's heart, as well as in your own heart. Embrace the next thirty-one days as you prayerfully go before God, your Heavenly Father. You can read straight from the text, you can say them out loud, you can get on your knees, or you can stand with your arms raised up towards the sky. You are God's daughter and He is going to be blessed hearing from you.

This is not a magical book that has any guarantee that your husband will change or that you will change once you reach day thirty-one. If you do not notice any change, please do not be disappointed or discouraged. I know there are some women who do not see the fruition of prayers until years, sometimes decades later, while others do not witness any change at all. Praying for your husband and your marriage requires faith, to believe even before you actually "see." It is imperative that you do not look to this book as a means to fix your husband or your marriage, but that above all else you trust in God whole-heartedly from now until the end of time!

My hope is that these prayers become a daily reminder for you to pray for your husband and your marriage. May you be blessed as you step into the Lord's throne room and petition for one of the most important relationships with which you have been gifted.

**I have included a few challenges to encourage you to think about the importance of prayer in your marriage. There are a total of 7 challenges for you to consider. I urge you to pray about each one and fulfill it when and how The Lord leads you!

***One last thing, I would love to see your journey along the way! If anything inspires you during this journey update social media and tag me @unveiledwife and #UW31Prayers so I can follow along!

Dear Heavenly Father,

I pray for the wife holding this book, getting ready to jump into thirty-one days of extraordinary with You. May Your Holy Spirit lead her through each prayer, adding to it personal needs of her husband. Anoint her and increase her faith as she puts her trust in You. Help her to surrender her desires for marriage and believe that You are moving. Give her the courage to fulfill each challenge and speak to her about when and how to carry each one out. May her husband be receptive and appreciative of her willingness to love him this way. I pray Your will be done in this marriage

in Jesus' name AMEN.

Leader Of The Home

Ephesians 5:23

Dear Lord,

Thank You for the gift of marriage and the beautiful way You have designed it. I value the different roles You have purposed for my husband and me. My hope is that we both continue to gain understanding in those different roles You have given to us. I pray for my husband today. May You fill him with Your peace and strip his heart of any worries. I pray You would mature my husband and mold him into the leader You have created him to be. Help him to be confident and faithful as a man of God. I pray You would anoint my husband, speak directly to him today, encourage him, and send other men to walk alongside him as positive examples of what it looks like to lead a family. I pray my husband is filled with compassion, gentleness, love, respect, and wisdom. Equip him to lead our family with boldness and integrity. I pray he will cherish me and lead me just as Christ leads His bride, the Church. I pray my husband grasps the responsibility he has as the head of our family, embracing his purpose, seeking diligently to fulfill all that You have called him to as a husband. I pray my husband will submit to You in humility as a servant, eager and willing to do Your will. May Your Holy Spirit lead him as he leads me in Jesus' name AMEN!

PERSONALIZE:

USE THIS AREA TO
WRITE A PERSONALIZED
PRAYER FOR YOUR
HUSBAND. YOU CAN
ALSO WRITE A LIST OF
THINGS YOU WOULD
LIKE TO CONTINUE TO
PRAY FOR.

His Job

Colossians 3:23-24

Dear God,

Thank You for the skills You have given to my husband. I pray he will be able to exercise those skills with passion in his job. I pray a blessing over him right now, asking You to anoint him today. Give my husband the strength to get through work joyfully and to be a blessing to others around him. Use him to benefit his company and to encourage the people he is working beside. May he be appreciated by his boss and other teammates. I pray my husband has an extraordinary day, that when he comes home he is excited to share with me all that took place. Lord, help me to be a good listener and help me to truly care about what he has endured throughout his time at work. If for any reason my husband desires a new job, I pray You would guide him and provide a job where he can thrive. Open new opportunities for my husband to consider and lead him to the perfect job. No matter what happens, please help both of us to trust in You as our ultimate provider and to appreciate where You have us at any given time! I pray my husband has a desire to serve You and to work unto You no matter what his job title states. I pray my husband will be willing to work extra hard and that You would reward him for his endeavors in Jesus' name AMEN!

PERSONALIZE:

Use this area to write a personalized prayer for your husband. You can also write a list of things you would like to continue to pray for.

Encouragement For Today

ROMANS 15:13

Dear Lord,

Thank You for this beautiful day. Thank You for my life and my husband's life. I pray my husband is encouraged in a major way today. May he sense You close as You reveal to him precious truths about who he is and what his future holds. May Your Holy Spirit teach him revelations about how to live according to Your ways, especially as a husband. Send people to give my husband verbal affirmations, notes describing his value, and a few compliments in the presence of his peers. May he open up Your word and read scripture after scripture detailing the great love You have for him. Let Your light shine brightly and show him just how much You care about every part of his life. I pray my husband feels respected and loved by all who surround him. Use me in any and every way You can to deeply touch his heart with encouragement in a profound way. I pray and hope our marriage is an encouragement to him as well. I pray he is satisfied in our relationship, yet excited for what lies ahead. Lift my husband up and remind him of his worth. My desire is that my husband trusts in You, Lord! Please fill his heart with joy and peace by the power of Your Holy Spirit and may he know that You are his source of life in Jesus' name AMEN!

USE THIS AREA TO WRITE A PERSONALIZED PRAYER FOR YOUR HUSBAND. YOU CAN ALSO WRITE A LIST OF THINGS YOU WOULD LIKE TO CONTINUE TO PRAY FOR.

Maturing My Husband
Ephesians 4:14-15

Dear Heavenly Father,

I love my husband with all my heart. Of course there are times when we disagree or even fight, but I do love my husband. My heart overflows with concern for him every day. I pray You would mature both of our characters and deepen our marriage relationship. I am confident that with You at the center of our relationship, my husband and I will continue to be blessed in our marriage, regardless of our faults and failures. Please help both of us to be willing to acknowledge our sin, repent, and strive for righteousness. I pray Your Holy Spirit would convict my husband's heart and redirect him to Your ways. I pray my husband will spend time searching Your holy word and submit to You in prayer. May his relationship with You grow exponentially. As he draws near to You, I know he will inevitably reflect Your awesome character. I pray against the enemy and the deceitful people the enemy uses to try to separate us from You, Lord. Bind the enemy in Jesus's name and protect my husband from being tossed back and forth by any kind of teaching or trend that is not of You! Guard his mind from believing lies, strengthen him by the truth of Your word. My desire is to see my husband mature in his relationship with You, to lean on Your understanding and not his own. Bless my husband as he strives to seek You in Jesus' name AMEN!

PERSONALIZE:

Use this area to write a personalized prayer for your husband. You can also write a list of things you would like to continue to pray for.

Challenge

START A PRAYER JOURNAL. ON ONE SIDE DATE AND WRITE YOUR PRAYER, AND ON THE OTHER SIDE DATE AND NOTE YOUR ANSWERED PRAYERS AS YOU RECEIVE THEM.

Relinquishing Worries

Psalm 55:22

Dear Lord,

You say in Your word not to worry, not to be afraid. I hope that my husband is not overwhelmed by anxiety, I pray he is not fearful of the future. My desire is that he can relinquish his worry and surrender it at the foot of Your throne. May You free him from any negative thoughts that threaten his heart and mind. May You pour out Your peace over him, that it may run over his body. Your amazing and transcending peace. Wrap him up in Your loving arms and comfort him. If there is anything pressing against him, anything stirring stress in his life, anything that triggers worry, I pray against it in Jesus's name. Free my husband from worry and build up his confidence for all that will come our way. Help me to be a comforter for my husband. I pray he lets me encourage him and receives my kind attempts to make things better. God, I pray my husband will trust You more and more each day, that he will walk by faith and lead by that faith. Strengthen my husband and keep his joy intact, for without joy our marriage suffers. Help both of us to discuss our worries and pray them away so that we do not react out of fear and accidently hurt each other. Please protect my husband from being oppressed by worry and sustain him completely in Jesus' name AMEN!

My Husband's Health

3 John 1:2

Dear Lord,

You are so amazing! Thank You for being a perfect example for my husband to look up to as a husband. I pray he will seek You daily to fully understand and grasp his role as my husband. I also ask that Your Holy Spirit would continue to refine him and draw him near to You. One specific area of his life I wanted to lift up to You today is my husband's health. It is so vital that he has great health so that he can take care of his family with joy and longevity. I do not want to see my husband suffer with illness or pain, but if he does, I hope he can find security in You still. My desire is for him to live a happy life, free of sickness or injury. I realize that diet and preventative care both play great big roles in maintaining his health, so I beg You to motivate my husband to pursue a healthy lifestyle. Help him to eat right, exercise, and get adequate rest. If he is stubborn, refusing to make healthy choices for his body, please convict his heart on the matter and help him to change. If my husband is suffering in any way, even if he has an issue that is affecting him, yet he remains unaware, would You please miraculously heal him completely. I pray my husband's health improves as he takes care of his body and his family in Jesus' name AMEN!

PERSONALIZE:

Use this area to write a personalized prayer for your husband. You can also write a list of things you would like to continue to pray for.

Exercising Self- Control

Proverbs 25:28

Dear Heavenly Father,

Being married is such a blessing to my life. I love my husband with all of my heart. I pray he has an incredible day, full of joy, laughter, and love. I also specifically pray and ask for You to help my husband to exercise self-control. Remind him how he should be walking and operating in the spirit and not the flesh. Empower him to say no to his flesh when temptations arise. I pray You would aid him in the words he chooses to use. May he share only what is needed to edify others. I pray he also exercises self-control when it comes to the food he consumes. Kindly nudge him to eat what is healthy for the nourishment of his body. In any circumstances that may confront my husband today, may he have the strength to surrender the reactions of his flesh and instead faithfully choose to react based on what You have taught him. May You retrain his mind and body so that he is not an impulsive man. With every decision he has to make today, may he be capable of submitting himself to You in humility. May he be patient enough to think through every step that he takes. As my husband is transformed in this area of his life, please keep his eyes open to the positive change and impact so that he is motivated to continue following You and Your mighty ways in Jesus' name Amen!

PERSONALIZE:

Use this area to write a personalized prayer for your husband. You can also write a list of things you would like to continue to pray for.

Challenge

Ask your husband to write down a list of specific prayer requests that he has, and refer to that list during the week as you pray for him. You can also add them to your prayer journal.

Grace in Marriage

HEBREWS 12:15

Dear Lord,

You know just how challenging marriage can be. My husband and I experience the ebb and flow of different emotions as we live together in this beautiful covenant of marriage. Our relationship has encountered both good times and more difficult times, joyful moments and painful moments. Yet all of it helps us to understand Your great love all the more! Our marriage specifically shows us the power of Your amazing grace. I pray that we are always humble enough to extend grace to each other. I pray that no root of bitterness will ever find a place in my husband's heart. For if there were no grace, our marriage would be full of trouble. Thank You Lord for Your gift of grace, for mercy and forgiveness. Thank You Jesus for exemplifying what grace should look like in marriage. Your grace has transformed my life, my husband's life, and it has transformed our marriage. I desire to have an intimate relationship with my husband where we can love extravagantly, be transparent with each other, and be quick to show grace to one another. May You help my husband to truly forgive me in the areas in which I am weak, and may we both be willing to reconcile during moments of conflict. Help my husband and me gift each other extraordinary love through the power of Your amazing grace in Jesus' name AMEN!

PERSONALIZE:

Use this area to write a personalized prayer for your husband. You can also write a list of things you would like to continue to pray for.

Pursuing Gentleness
Ephesians 4:2-3

Dear Heavenly Father,

I lift up my husband to You today and ask that You would teach him how to be more gentle with me. Fill my husband with a desire to treat me and others with compassion and thoughtfulness. I realize that sometimes I can be a sensitive wife; however, regardless of whether I am being sensitive or not, I believe a strong and caring man should value the art of gentleness. Soothe his touch, soften his tone, brighten his eyes, open the gates of his heart and let gentleness pour out of him. I long to be cherished and I long to be valued, which my husband does do. However, I want it to be more natural for him to fulfill those needs of mine as he intentionally seeks to be gentle with me. Humble his heart and help him to be patient with me. I pray my husband is quick to make every effort he can to keep the unity of The Spirit through the bond of peace in our marriage. Holy Spirit, please cultivate a desire in my husband's heart to want to be gentle towards me. Inspire him to make changes in how he does things to incorporate more lovingkindness. I also pray that I will be gentle toward my husband, especially in the way in which I communicate with him. Let gentleness be a fruit that flows from both of us, positively affecting our lives in a powerful way in Jesus' name AMEN!

Confidence

Hebrews 10:35-36

Dear God,

Thank You for Your incredible provision. I appreciate the life You have given to me and my husband. Thank You for the hope You have filled us with. I am in awe of Your great love for me and my family. I also thank You for my husband. I pray for him today as he goes about his business. May You give him an increase of confidence. May he know Your will for his life, may he have passion to fulfill Your purpose for him, and may he experience growth in his faith every single day. I pray that whether he is facing a battle, enduring work, investing in friendships, tending to his family, or taking a moment to show kindness to strangers, may he be motivated by the confidence he has in You. Lord, I ask that You would gift my husband courage to love extravagantly and to share Your Gospel by the way he lives his life. Feed my husband's faith and confident heart with Your words of wisdom and encouragement. Lead him through scripture, impressing on him verses that will contribute to the growth of confidence and courage. I pray he would fight for justice, never allowing evil to intimidate him or others. Please help my husband to stand strong, to persevere, and to do Your will. May he be a man of honor, a man undaunted, a man who fears only You in Jesus' name AMEN!

PERSONALIZE:

Use this area to write a personalized prayer for your husband. You can also write a list of things you would like to continue to pray for.

Forgiving His Sin
MATTHEW 6:14-15

Dear God,

I lift up my relationship with my husband to You right now. I know that he struggles with his own personal sin and I know You are transforming him. Sometimes I get hurt by his sin. It affects me in huge ways. This makes it all the more difficult to forgive him. However, You have given me grace for my sins even when I hurt You. Thank You for forgiveness and thank You for grace and mercy. I pray that I will be able to forgive my husband as You have forgiven me. Help me to extend grace to him. Help me to see him as the man he is being transformed into, a man You desire him to be. Thank You, Lord, for helping me to overcome the hurt and pain of my husband's sin. Thank You for helping me to forgive him and experience true healing. I realize that my sin also hurts my husband. Please help me to stop sinning against him. I pray my husband will have compassion on me and forgive me as well. I ask that You would heal my husband of any wounds I have caused him. I implore Your Holy Spirit to teach him the deep meaning of forgiveness and the power it has to reconcile us. I pray my husband and I will be humble, willing to apologize and forgive often, and eager to restore any brokenness we cause in our relationship because of sin. May You continue to protect our marriage and our intimacy in Jesus' name AMEN!

PERSONALIZE:
Use this area to write a personalized prayer for your husband. You can also write a list of things you would like to continue to pray for.

Challenge

SPONTANEOUSLY ASK YOUR HUSBAND IF YOU CAN PRAY FOR HIM. HOLD HANDS WHILE YOU PRAY OUT LOUD.

Freedom from Lust

1 John 2:16

Dear Lord,

My husband was designed by Your amazing creativeness. He was given eyes that see, a mind that focuses, and a heart that is full of desire. I pray that these gifts, his eyes, his mind, and his heart, will be intimately directed toward me. Please remove any pollution that may have stained any of these areas. Prune any pathways that were forged by sin. I pray You would destroy any passion for lust in my husband, anything that would cause him to stumble. May You restore his gifts so that no matter how I age or mature he desires only me, finds me attractive, and remains passionate about our relationship. Please protect my husband from his flesh and the parts of him susceptible to corruption. There are so many ways this world can pervert beauty or use sex to sell. I pray against this. I pray against the lust of the flesh. Cover my husband in righteousness and fill him with self-control so that he can stand firm against temptation. Give him eyes to see me and the beauty of our relationship. Help my husband unlearn some of the habits he has formed, and retrain him to find pleasure in the wholeness of our marriage. I pray that our sexual intimacy stimulates both of us and satisfies our flesh in a healthy way in Jesus' name AMEN!

PERSONALIZE:

Use this area to write a personalized prayer for your husband. You can also write a list of things you would like to continue to pray for.

Cultivating Romance

SONG OF SOLOMON 1:2

Dear Heavenly Father,

My husband and I rush to check off our to-do lists, easily forgetting or neglecting the truth that we are married, and that we need to cultivate romance in our relationship. I pray You would inspire my husband to initiate romantically in our marriage. May he pursue me as if I were his greatest priority, after You, of course. My heart yearns to connect with my husband amidst the busy in our days. Inspire creative ways for him to show me his love and adoration. I also pray that I will have the courage and energy to bless him and pursue him romantically. Lord, please provide the time and resources for us to date each other for the rest of our lives. I pray we will always be willing to look at each other with fire in our eyes and passion oozing from our hearts for one another. May our physical affections satisfy us completely. I pray my husband never feels overwhelmed or stressed when it comes to cultivating romance, but rather he finds every opportunity as a precious gift given by You, a gift we must take advantage of daily. Help my husband to love me extravagantly and help me to respond respectfully every time. Lord, I pray that my husband will go out of his way to show me I am worthy. Also, help him understand how his touch lets me know he is near and there for me. Stir in my husband a motivation to speak my love language in Jesus' name AMEN!

PERSONALIZE:

Use this area to write a personalized prayer for your husband. You can also write a list of things you would like to continue to pray for.

Knowing His Purpose

ROMANS 8:28

Dear Lord,

I pray that my husband knows his purpose in life. Reveal to him what You desire him to do. My husband is a man of many talents, a man of skills, a man of worthiness, a man with ability, and a man with a heart to fulfill purpose. I pray my husband will receive supernatural confidence, a motivator to help him follow through with anything You ask of him. I pray that his ears are sensitive to Your voice and that he has such an intimate relationship with You that he never misses an invitation to join You. I pray my husband will have the courage to fulfill his purpose in life. I also pray You would satisfy his longing to matter to others, his longing to be recognized for the things he does, and his longing to do something extraordinary. I pray his whole life is extraordinary and that he sees it that way. Holy Spirit, please remove any ounce of complaint from my husband so that he does not miss out on fulfilling his purpose. I implore You, Lord, to guard my husband's life and defend him against the enemy as he seeks to love You and do Your will. Clarify the calling You have for my husband and equip him so that he may be a good and faithful servant in Jesus' name AMEN!

PERSONALIZE:

Use this area to write a personalized prayer for your husband. You can also write a list of things you would like to continue to pray for.

Patience

1 Corinthians 13:4-8

Dear Father,

I pray over my husband and ask that You would fill his heart and cover his mind with patience. I pray nothing will make him frustrated or stressed out today. May Your Holy Spirit mold my husband and shape him to have incredible amounts of endurance and perseverance. I pray he will always be slow to anger. Lord, may You help my husband have self-control with his emotions as well as his reaction to every situation. Show my husband how to remain calm no matter what circumstances he faces. May my husband's countenance and composure reflect the character of Christ, the compassion, the understanding, and the grace. I pray my husband treats others with the utmost love and respect. If there is an area of his life that causes contention or tests his patience often, I pray You would help him to exercise that particular fruit of The Spirit. Also, please reveal to my husband when he does have more patience in those times of tension, so that he will be encouraged to press on ahead with a joyful attitude. I especially pray that my husband will be patient with me as we continue to learn how to be on the same team in our marriage. I pray he chooses to be kind and gentle toward me, protecting our relationship through his behavior in Jesus' name AMEN!

Challenge

Invite your husband to pray with you every morning to get your day started with God at the center.

Gaining More Wisdom

JAMES 1:5

Dear Lord,

Thank You for my husband's life. Thank You for teaching him and maturing him over the years. Thank You for revealing great truths to him. I love watching him grow into the man I know You created him to be. I pray You would continue to richly bless my husband with Your wisdom. Giving him knowledge and sharing with him deep understanding is important, but wisdom is the ability to apply such information. I pray my husband will apply what he knows he should. Help my husband to put into action the very convictions You have impressed upon his heart and mind. Holy Spirit, please continue to guide my husband, leading him with Your divine insight. God, I ask that You would continue to give wisdom to my husband generously, that he will know and do right in every situation. I pray the wisdom You give him positively impacts our marriage, building my trust in him, and ultimately increasing our intimacy. Protect my husband from the enemy, the one who is on the prowl to steal any bit of wisdom You give. Defend my husband and help him to stand as a man of integrity, a man of righteousness, a man of intelligence, a man who does Your will, and a man who strives to be a great husband in Jesus' name AMEN!

Protecting Our Marriage

2 Thessalonians 3:3

Dear Lord,

I humbly pray for my husband today. There are many times I have the urge to reprimand or try to fix my husband, yet I am learning that I am not a substitute for Your Holy Spirit. Only You have the power to transform my husband. So I submit my grievances and desires to You and ask that You would radically transform my husband. He is a good man and I love him more than anyone else in this world. I desire the best for him and for our marriage. I implore You to protect our marriage. Strengthen the areas of our relationship that are weak, the parts that are vulnerable to attack or temptation. I pray that my husband and I can build up our marriage together and fight for our love every single day. I pray against evil, I pray against the lust of our flesh, I pray against anything and everything that threatens what we have. Please Lord, wrap us up in Your loving and strong arms and guard us against the flaming arrows of the evil one. May Your Holy Spirit strengthen us each day and remind us to intentionally invest in our marriage. You are so faithful, Lord! I am so thankful You have carried us through some of the most challenging circumstances we have ever encountered. Please continue to show us how to keep our eyes focused on You in Jesus' name AMEN!

PERSONALIZE:

Use this area to write a personalized prayer for your husband. You can also write a list of things you would like to continue to pray for.

My Husband's Needs

PHILIPPIANS 4:19

Dear Lord,

It can be so easy for me to get my feelings hurt if my needs are not met by my husband. At times I even use my prayers as a means to complain. I am so sorry, Lord! I apologize for being so selfish and I repent of being so self-focused. Please give me eyes to see my husband's needs and to sincerely care about their fulfillment. Motivate my heart to do all that I can for him. Help me to be a wife who seeks to please her husband, who refuses laziness, who continually serves extravagantly so that I may brightly shine the love of Christ. I pray for my husband's needs right now. May You graciously meet all of his needs and use me to also help fulfill them. I pray he receives affirmation today, I pray he receives recognition and respect, I pray we come together intimately, I pray he experiences satisfaction, and I pray he feels accomplished. If he feels as if he is lacking anything, may You supply and satisfy him. May You bless him with good company, a warm meal, love, and moments of enlightenment. It would be so amazing to hear my husband mention how complete he feels, how loved he feels, and how cherished he feels by You and by me. May today be the day I hear him relish in contentment in Jesus' name AMEN!

PERSONALIZE:

Use this area to write a personalized prayer for your husband. You can also write a list of things you would like to continue to pray for.

A Servant's Heart
MATTHEW 20:25-28

Dear Heavenly Father,

Thank You for sending Your Son to save the world! There are no words to describe the joy in my heart to know that Christ came to save me, to save my husband. Jesus Christ lived a perfect life and exemplified how we should live. I pray that my husband and I can serve each other and love each other just like Him. May You transform our hearts so that we always think like Jesus, intentionally serving others compassionately. It would be so awesome to experience more intimacy in my marriage, and I believe that is a result of serving one another. I pray my husband has a servant's heart. May he be willing to step up and help others in need. Give my husband courage to approach those he feels may need a hand, even if he doesn't know them or if they never ask for help. I pray that I and others will receive my husband's help with gratefulness. Put passion in my husband's heart to go the extra mile, to love without conditions, to radically impact lives through grace and generosity. I pray that as my husband serves, I will also learn to have a servant's heart. May we teach each other and remind each other daily to seek to bless those around us. I am so excited to make my marriage reflect Christ's love through our choices both great and small. Lord, may You be glorified through us in Jesus' name AMEN!

PERSONALIZE:

Use this area to write a personalized prayer for your husband. You can also write a list of things you would like to continue to pray for.

Use My Husband

Ephesians 2:10

Dear Lord,

My husband was created to do good works. I am confident that You have prepared these works in advance and You have known his purpose from the beginning. I am full of joy knowing that You have built my husband to do specific things, and I pray I can support him in fulfilling those things. I pray Your will be done in his life. Lord, I also am confident that You paired us together, joining us as one to do great things. May You open our eyes and impress upon our hearts the desires You have for our marriage. Whisper in our ears and shout from Your Heavenly throne every step we should take in whichever direction You want to lead us. Holy Spirit, guide us as we choose to follow You every day. I specifically ask that You inspire my husband to work joyfully unto You. Use him in mighty ways to draw others toward You, to show others Your love and grace, to comfort others in their pain, to encourage others in Your purpose for their lives. I also pray my husband can do this in our marriage. May he love me like Jesus, may he show me compassion, and may he support me in my purpose. My heart's desire is that we both, as Your handiwork, fulfill the extraordinary plans You have prepared for us and our marriage in Jesus' name AMEN!

PERSONALIZE:

Use this area to write a personalized prayer for your husband. You can also write a list of things you would like to continue to pray for.

Challenge

Spend time praying with your husband right before engaging in sexual intimacy. Pray that God blesses your time together.

Making Good Choices
PROVERBS 16:3

Dear Heavenly Father,

I try to make good decisions. I desire to make good decisions. However, sometimes I am weak, I slip, I fail, I am unwise. Thank You for Your grace and forgiveness. I am forever grateful. I pray for Your wisdom to guide me, that Your Holy Spirit helps me make good decisions for my life, my marriage, and my family. I also pray that You would anoint my husband so that he will also make good decisions, especially as he leads our family. Whether he is at work, having fun with friends, at the grocery store, using the Internet or television, spending time with me or with family, doing an activity, or driving down the street, no matter what my husband is doing, I pray he will choose to live righteously. Holy Spirit, please move in his heart, speak to him, guide him. Help him to remain pure and holy. May You fill my husband with wisdom and help him apply Your wisdom throughout the day. Every decision he makes has a ripple effect in our marriage, and I desire that he understands the weight of responsibility he has as the leader of our home. Let joy parade in his heart over this responsibility. I pray that as we are faced with decisions together, we can encourage each other to make good decisions based on Your words and ways in Jesus' name AMEN!

PERSONALIZE:

Use this area to write a personalized prayer for your husband. You can also write a list of things you would like to continue to pray for.

Discernment

PSALM 119:125

Dear Lord,

I believe that having discernment is vital. It is the gift of judging well, the ability to know right from wrong, the understanding of good and evil. My husband encounters situations every moment of every day where discernment is needed. In our marriage alone it is important for him to be able to judge a circumstance and choose wisely what to do about it. I also know that discernment will not be his strength unless he understands Your word, Your ways. I pray You would give my husband an intense passion and desire to read Your word. May he find time every day to commit to prayer and reading scripture. I also ask that You provide understanding with every word of Yours that he reads. Let each verse sink deeply into his soul and be written on his heart. As he seeks You and learns Your word, he will better grasp Your statutes, comprehend what it means to be Your servant, and behold his role as a husband. I desire my husband to be a man of honor, a man of righteousness, a man after Your own heart! Thank You for my husband and thank You for pursuing him so intimately. I pray that he reciprocates Your love and joins Your invitation to live out an extraordinary life full of joy and led by discernment in Jesus' name AMEN!

PERSONALIZE:

Use this area to write a personalized prayer for your husband. You can also write a list of things you would like to continue to pray for.

Protection Over Him

Romans 12:2

Dear Lord,

Thank You for my husband. Thank You for hearing my prayers and thank You for moving in our marriage. I pray protection over my husband's heart and mind today. Our culture seems to accept explicit sexual content for marketing and my husband is subject to this way of advertising. Guard him against this by removing this content from the places he travels on a daily basis. Divert his eyes to Your beauty and Your truth. I pray against advertisements that pop up on his screen, in his email, or anywhere else whether online or in public. Give my husband the strength to look away and then inspire him to pray against the enemy's attacks. Also, inspire him to pray for our culture, to fight for more modesty, for more purity. I pray my husband is a warrior for You, Lord, a warrior that prayerfully overcomes the temptation of lust. I also pray for my husband to be equipped with wisdom so that his heart and mind do not convince him to stray from Your ways. Protect him from thinking badly about others, from assuming the worst instead of searching for truth, and from choosing unrighteousness. Renew my husband so that he would not conform to this world. In all he does, may he glorify You and honor our marriage in Jesus' name AMEN!

PERSONALIZE:

Use this area to write a personalized prayer for your husband. You can also write a list of things you would like to continue to pray for.

Sexual Intimacy

Hebrews 13:4

Dear Lord,

I pray for my marriage. I pray specifically for my sex life. I ask that You would help me to improve sexual intimacy in my marriage. Sometimes I am not in the mood. Sometimes we avoid each other because of laziness or some other distractions. I am sure there is something I can do to help make it better. Often I just want my husband to do everything or make the changes in our relationship, but I am aware that I have responsibilities, too. I want to be a wife who can fulfill her husband in all areas, including sexual intimacy. May You bless this part of our marriage and may my husband and I both put the effort in to improve it. I pray my husband will have an insatiable desire for me. Inspire him with creative ways to pursue me romantically. Reveal to my husband how he can satisfy my heart completely. Help us to communicate what we like and what we would like to improve or change. I pray my husband and I will grow together in this area of intimacy as we make ourselves fully known to each other. Break us free from any strongholds that keep us down. Break our perspectives and our thoughts of unrealistic expectations. Help us to honor our relationship and help us to keep our marriage bed pure in Jesus' name AMEN!

Challenge

INVITE YOUR HUSBAND TO PRAY WITH YOU ABOUT HOW GOD WOULD WANT YOU TOGETHER TO BLESS A FAMILY IN NEED. THEN AT SOME TIME DURING THE DAY, DO WHAT YOU BOTH FEEL LED TO DO FOR THAT FAMILY.

Filled With Compassion

1 Peter 3:8

Dear Heavenly Father,

Please fill my husband with compassion, the deep, awe-inspiring compassion that makes up the heart of Jesus. I pray my husband will feel strongly sympathetic for others. Help him to be like-minded so that he can have great understanding for other people and their circumstances. I pray that my husband would also have incredible compassion with me. May his love for me be deeply rooted in his heart. Humble my husband and guide him as he interacts with people throughout his day. Whisper to him and teach him how to comfort, provide for, be sympathetic towards, and bring aid to those in need. But also, provide him with structure and boundaries so that no one takes advantage of him or our marriage. I pray those whom he helps would never see his compassion as a desire to form any type of relationship that would compromise his vows of marriage. I know that my husband cares for me and cares for others. I admire this about him and I pray that his compassion only grows. Inspire my husband and use him to fulfill Your will of drawing people in to know the heart of Jesus. May Your Holy Spirit anoint my husband and use him to do great and mighty things for You in Jesus' name AMEN!

PERSONALIZE:

Use this area to write a personalized prayer for your husband. You can also write a list of things you would like to continue to pray for.

Building Strong Friendships

PROVERBS 11:14

Dear God,

It is becoming increasingly evident to me that You value relationships. I pray my husband and I also value relationships. May we cultivate a strong relationship in our marriage, but also help us build up strong friendships with other couples who can lift us up and point us toward You. I pray my husband and I can be awesome friends to others and lead them as well. I pray my husband finds authentic friendships with other men, other husbands, who strive to live righteously. As my husband sees these examples in real life, I know he will be inspired to continually grow in the roles and responsibilities You have given to him. Put people in close proximity to him who will keep him accountable and care about the issues he faces. May these friends encourage him and may he be a blessing to them as well. I pray that as a couple we connect with other couples, where we can talk about marriage issues and discuss Your glorious design of marriage. I pray these friends challenge us, cry with us, laugh with us, and experience life with us. May these friends help guide us and advise us with the important decisions we encounter, as well as the smaller ones that have great implications, such as how we love each other. Thank You for my husband and the opportunity we have to be great friends to each other. My prayer is that we seek peace and unity always in Jesus' name AMEN!

Strength for My Husband

ISAIAH 41:10

Dear God,

I pray for my husband right now. I pray You would anoint him with marvelous strength. I pray he physically feels great today, capable of doing any work You have set before him. I pray for his mind, that You would keep him focused and safeguard him from the temptation of lust. I pray his heart will dwell on You and that he will be joyful and content. I pray he will carry a smile on his face! May You send him encouragement throughout the day and use me to affirm him. Send others to encourage him as well. Lord, I ask that my husband will not be dismayed or overwhelmed by any circumstances. Please uphold him with Your righteous right hand. May he know You as his God and may he draw close to You. If he feels at all unworthy or undervalued, I pray You would lift him up. If he feels discouraged, I ask that Your Holy Spirit remind him of what You believe about him. Reinforce in his heart and mind how valuable he is and equip him with energy. I also ask that You provide endurance for him, especially as a husband, so that together we may persevere. Bless my husband in great ways and increase his faith and confidence in Jesus' name AMEN!

Breaking Strongholds

1 Corinthians 15:57

Dear God,

My heart is in anguish. My husband is a good man, yet he faces so many struggles. This breaks my heart. I am sure he even battles issues I do not know fully. Please break down the strongholds that have reached out and grabbed my husband. I pray against the temptations that seek to pull him away from You and away from our marriage. Never let me forget or neglect to fight for my husband through prayer. I believe there is power in these prayers and I believe You hear me when I ask You to intercede for my husband. I have faith that extraordinary things happen when prayer is made a priority. I pray that You would strengthen my husband, bolster his faith, fill him with courage and wisdom, and equip him to fight against the strongholds that call out to him or grab for his heart. I claim the power of Jesus and the transforming grace You have gifted to us and I pray my husband will never slip or falter. Yet if he does, may You carry him to safety. Be his refuge and salvation. Help my husband to truly believe he is set free in Jesus. Reveal to my husband the freedom and victory he already has in his life because of Christ. Holy Spirit, I call upon Your name to step in and save my husband from sin, redeem and restore him, and rewire his heart and mind so that he will live as a mighty warrior for You and for me in Jesus' name AMEN!

Goodbye Pride

PROVERBS 11:2

Dear Lord,

When pride come so does disgrace. I do not want my husband to be a man or a husband of disgrace. I desire my husband to be respected by all, which requires him to lay down his pride and let humility lead his life. May You teach him the importance of humility, as well as what it looks like to be motivated in every decision by humility. I believe others would be inspired to see my husband as confident and faithful, but not puffed up or arrogant. I also know I would be much more attracted to him when pride is pruned from his heart because I have seen him this way before. When my heart recognizes the character of Christ in my husband, I can't help but be all the more attracted to him. I specifically pray against pride in our marriage. Having a prideful posture leads to self-preservation instead of protecting us as one. Help both of us to respond and react to each other with kindness and compassion. I pray my husband can say goodbye to pride, laying it at the foot of Your throne. Open his eyes and reveal to my husband if there are parts of his heart where pride is taking up residence. Strip him of arrogance and the need to be right. Fill him with a desire to be a peace seeker and an ambassador for unity in Jesus' name AMEN!

PERSONALIZE:

Use this area to write a personalized prayer for your husband. You can also write a list of things you would like to continue to pray for.

Integrity

Proverbs 10:9

Dear God,

Thank You for my husband and the way that he loves me. Thank You for joining us together as one. I pray we grow closer together and experience deeper intimacy as we let down our walls, allowing us to get to truly know one another. I lift up my husband to You, asking that he will be a man of integrity. May his life be a testament of Your Gospel, a lighthouse for others, leading them to Your love. I pray against any urge he may have to lie, make excuses, defend himself for actions that are not honorable, or justify any behavior that is contrary to Your word. I implore Your Holy Spirit to radically transform my husband and lead him every day. I pray my husband chooses to walk a secure path, a way that pleases You. I pray he fears You and only You, Lord. As my husband walks in integrity, I am confident that our trust will be built upon, our relationship made incredibly stronger. Teach my husband what is true, right, worthy, and pure. Reveal to him the significance of honesty in marriage. Convict his heart on this matter so that he will desire to strive for righteousness. I also ask that You would cover my husband and protect him from any influence that would tempt him in any direction that would lure him away from You. Shield my husband's mind and heart so that his integrity stays intact in Jesus' name AMEN!

PERSONALIZE:

Use this area to write a personalized prayer for your husband. You can also write a list of things you would like to continue to pray for.

Challenge

ASK YOUR HUSBAND IF YOU CAN PRAY SPECIFICALLY FOR HIM. LAY YOUR HANDS ON HIM WHEREVER YOU FEEL COMFORTABLE, AND BEGIN BY ASKING THE HOLY SPIRIT TO LEAD YOU. THEN TAKE A FEW MOMENTS, UNINTERRUPTED, TO PRAY FOR YOUR HUSBAND.

Extraordinary Marriage

Mark 10:6-9

Dear Heavenly Father,

Thank You for my marriage. I am so blessed to have my husband, my lover, my friend. Regardless of the conflict we face, the trials and challenges, my marriage is a gift from You, a gift I embrace every day. I pray protection over my marriage. I ask that You would protect us from our selfish ways. Mature us and refine us so that we can help each other through this life together. I also pray protection against the schemes of the enemy, who seeks to destroy what You have created. May You bind the enemy in Jesus's name! Holy Spirit, cover us and anoint our marriage. Break any strongholds in our lives and break our heart for what breaks Yours. Let compassion rule in our hearts! God, I ask that my husband and I will experience an extraordinary marriage. I pray our intimacy thrives, our communication is clear, our companionship a priority, and our relationship a reflection of Your incredible love story. As we are united and joined as one flesh, may our hearts yearn to keep the sanctity of our vows a motivator in our every response to each other. I pray You would move in my husband's heart and help me to see how You are moving in our marriage. I submit to You, Lord! I submit my marriage to You as well. May Your will be done in us and through us in Jesus' name AMEN!

PERSONALIZE:

Use this area to write a personalized prayer for your husband. You can also write a list of things you would like to continue to pray for.

A Letter From

Jennifer Smith

Dear Friend,

I commend you for diligently praying through this book. For putting your husband's needs above your own and petitioning for him before God. Do not let this be the last time you pick up this book and use the prayers to guide you. This is your resource and one that I hope you will hold closely to your heart. May you also recognize this as just a resource to help draw you closer to God, but may you fully understand that there is no greater closeness to God than reading His Word! I urge you to spend intentional time reading the Bible daily and continue to pray and communicate with God!

I would love to hear all about what you experienced along this journey! You can always submit a post to social media, tag me @unveiledwife, and share so that I can see and other wives can be encouraged! Be sure to also add **#UW31Prayers** so that we can all follow the conversations as other wives around the world participate in praying for their husbands!

Never give up praying for your husband and for your marriage! Go before God and share with Him your heart and all that you feel on a daily basis. Pray in faith for reconciliation and transformation for you and for your husband. Persevere my friend!

GRAB A COPY OF MY NEW BOOK "THE UNVEILED WIFE" WHERE I TALK ABOUT HOW GOD GOT A HOLD OF MY HEART DURING THE HARDEST TIME IN MY MARRIAGE.

UNVEILEDWIFEBOOK.COM

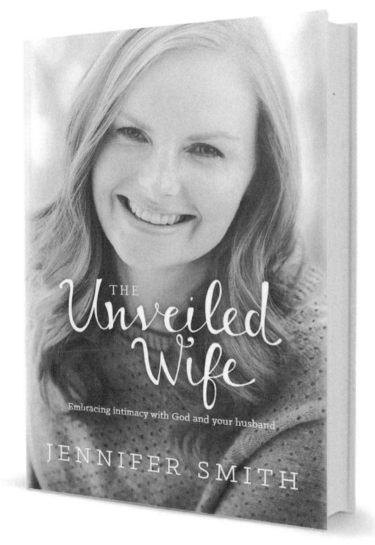

THE

Unveiled Wife

Embracing intimacy with God and your husband

JENNIFER SMITH

If this prayer book has blessed you please consider picking up a copy of my 30 day devotional and support the Unveiled Wife community.

WifeAfterGod.com

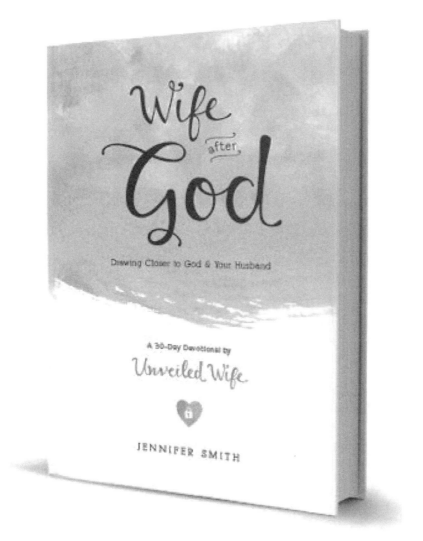

Wife
after
God

Drawing Closer to God & Your Husband

A 30-Day Devotional by

Unveiled Wife

JENNIFER SMITH

Order My Book Today
UnveiledWifeBook.com

Get The Unveiled Wife Devotionals:
WifeAfterGod.com

For more marriage resources please visit:
unveiledwife.com/marriage-resources/

Receive daily prayer for your marriage via email:
unveiledwife.com/daily-prayer/

Get connected:
Facebook.com/unveiledwife
Pinterest.com/unveiledwife
Youtube.com/unveiledwife
Instagram.com/unveiledwife
Twitter.com/unveiledwife